VOCAL IMPROVISATION

CHECK FOR CD

Edited by Jonathan Feist

BOB STOLOFF

Berklee Press

Vice President of Berklee Media: David Kusek
Vice President of Berklee Media: Debbie Cavalier
Assistant Vice President/CFO of Berklee Media: Robert F. Green
Managing Editor: Jonathan Feist
Editorial Assistants: Martin Fowler, David Hume, Amy Kaminsky,
Ben Scudder, Jacqueline Sim, Won (Sara) Hwang
Cover Designer: Kathy Kikkert

ISBN 978-0-87639-102-0

DISTRIBUTED BY

1140 Boylston Street
Boston, MA 02215-3693 USA
(617) 747-2146

Visit Berklee Press Online at
www.berkleepress.com

HAL•LEONARD®
CORPORATION
7777 W. BLUEMOUND RD. P.O. BOX 13819
MILWAUKEE, WISCONSIN 53213

Visit Hal Leonard Online at
www.halleonard.com

CONTENTS

CD TRACKS

INTRODUCTION

Teaching vocalists to improvise has been my passion since I decided to become a music teacher forty years ago. As a trained instrumentalist on trumpet, flute, drums, and bass, I never expected to be a worldwide mentor of vocal jazz and improvisation, yet here I am coaching singers in the art of solo scat and group improvisation with much success!

There was a brief period when I felt that all the years I practiced trumpet etudes and drum rudiments were a sacrifice of additional time I could have devoted to vocal training, until I discovered that singers, like myself, like to emulate musical instruments. I also realized that many of the techniques I had learned playing them could be applied with equal success to the voice. This "instru-vocal" approach to singing evolved into an alternative method of improvisation pedagogy purely by coincidence.

While solo scat singing has been around for many years, the idea of vocalists improvising in groups is still relatively new. The concept was introduced by Rhiannon, explored by Joey Blake and Bobby McFerrin's Voicestra, and is currently the focal point of Roger Treece's recently recorded vocal arrangements of McFerrin's improvisations. My own contribution to communal singing reflects the experiences I had playing in bands, orchestras, and studio rhythm sections where teamwork and cooperation were always essential.

Vocal Improvisation represents a culmination of my years teaching at Berklee and presenting vocal improvisation seminars throughout the United States and Europe. All the exercises and activities I've included are intended for a diverse range of musical backgrounds and experience. Learning to improvise should be fun, so I hope you enjoy this book!

CHAPTER 1

Music in Motion

As an instru-vocal instructor, I have spent the last thirty-five years teaching musicians how to improvise using their voice as a musical instrument. My experience includes mentoring vocalists of various stylistic backgrounds and levels of training.

All have had in common a chronic fear, not just of improvising but also of the vocal sound and expression they are capable of producing. This distinguishes the vocalist from the instrumentalist in that, physically, their voice is their instrument. There is an expectation by singers that their voices should sound as aesthetic, good, or even as "perfect" as a musical instrument.

It is from observing and working with this anxiety that I originated the following nontraditional activities to help people discover the innate qualities of their voice and to enjoy the experience of singing with minimal self-judgment. The "music in motion" exercises in this chapter are designed to increase the singer's comfort level and self-esteem while easing them into the world of improvisation. They are intended to be fun!

Other than the icebreaker song, all the activities allow the singer the freedom to make whatever sounds they want, instead of more traditional exercises, like trying to match pitch or read music. They are all in a follow-the-leader format, which gives an easy framework for generating and structuring improvisational ideas, and they will help you to discover your voice and improvisational style.

While these exercises may be accomplished by individuals practicing alone, I highly recommend using a group format, if possible. Becoming accustomed to group improvisation reduces the self-consciousness singers often feel when performing in front of one another. Additionally, this kind of group exercise encourages a sense of community, which vocalists thrive on. From my experience, discovering your voice is the first step toward realizing improvisation!

Activity 1.1. Icebreaker Song

Folks are often very intimidated by the idea of "making up" music, and this fear runs deep. If you are in a situation where you or some other singer is intimidated by the idea of improvising, it's a good idea to begin a session by singing a simple, comfortable, and fun tune as an icebreaker. Whether you are singing with a band or leading a group where others are improvising, this is a good way to begin.

I often use this exercise when I lead group improvisation workshops. Many of the participants are improvising for the first time, and I want this initial experience to be a good one. As a nonthreatening gesture, I always initiate my introductory session by singing a popular song—something perhaps from a television show or an equally familiar, simple, fun tune that will serve as an impetus for the group to bond with you as facilitator and with the others in the group.

I love using the "SpongeBob SquarePants" theme, because all my Berklee students know the song, it's riddled with call-and-response, and the audience part is one line repeatedly shouted in unison. A perfect icebreaker! (I also punctuate my sessions with imitations of Patrick and Mr. Krabs—two of the characters in this famous cartoon.) It also takes the group by surprise, because people usually expect some kind of formal introduction to classes, clinics, sessions, or workshops and will retreat emotionally at the slightest provocation or feeling of risk.

The humor and lightness of this type of activity should increase the comfort zone of most if not all the participants. It will also get them excited about the session and to hopefully feel open to the magic of improvisation you're going to introduce! If everyone is having fun, how threatening could it be?

Activity 1.2. Soundtrack

Using the voice to produce sound should be a natural event, and yet there always seems to be a tendency to experience feelings of self-consciousness, especially in group situations. However, both experienced and novice singers seem to respond well to the "Soundtrack" exercise, when practiced in a communal or collective group format where participants are free to create sounds, initially in unison, without the expectation of producing "organized" music, which may be subject to critique. Though intended for groups, this exercise can also be practiced alone simply by following the instructions below and initiating your own vocal sounds to your own motions.

In "Soundtrack," the leader moves his or her body using everything from conducting motions to subjective body movements using hands, arms, feet, and torso. The group provides a collective "score" or "soundtrack" based on each motion, spontaneously creating, in a sense, background "music" for a silent film to use an appropriate example. You probably did this as a child.

This ambience is not music in the traditional sense but rather spontaneous vocal sound effects, which will contain traditional musical components later on with some additional training.

Making a connection between vocal sound and motion is intended to further alleviate the fear of singing, and it has proven to be another good icebreaker exercise. Furthermore, creating individual vocal sounds in a group format removes the tendency for anyone to feel self-conscious about their particular voice timbre, articulation ability, etc.

Activity 1.3. Snake

Wavy snake-like arm/hand motions are articulated by the leader/conductor to evoke a dissonant drone that moves between high and low pitches as cued. Varying speed and/or direction will translate to musical ideas with a variety of articulation possibilities.

Activity 1.4. Imaginary Ball

Using the art of mime, the leader pretends to hold an invisible object that can be changed at will to create musical variations, similar in effect to the exercises described above. I usually start this activity by simulating a spinning ball using a twirling motion with one hand while "holding" the ball with the other.

The leader holds one hand out, palm up, fingers slightly curled upward as if balancing an imaginary ball (any size). He or she uses the other hand to initiate a spinning motion, and continues holding the "spinning ball." Then, the leader begins to play with the ball, throwing it up in the air and catching it, perhaps occasionally stopping the spinning motion, but always keeping the ball "in play" even between motions.

I will often "spin" the ball on one finger, like a seal might on his nose, and go back and forth between each hand.

The leader might have to initiate this exercise by making his or her own sounds to suggest the rules of the game without having to verbally explain what to do. But if done with conviction (and humor), the intention of this exercise should be obvious.

Regardless of group size, it is always exciting to hand the "ball" to a willing participant, inviting them to continue while the "voicestra" continues to match their particular motions with improvised vocal sounds. Some people like to make their own sounds, and this is perfectly okay for the group to just observe. If the individual starts motioning in silence, that's usually an unspoken cue for the group to provide accompaniment. Other motions to consider: dribbling a basketball, kicking a football, throwing a baseball, flinging a Frisbee, tossing a boomerang, unfurling a bowling ball, swinging at a tennis ball, jumping rope, boxing a punching bag, kicking a field goal, swinging a golf club, martial arts, etc.

> **NOTE:** A great way to end this activity is to "inflate" the ball until it explodes, pop a hole to "deflate" it, or perhaps hurl it upward into oblivion.

Activity 1.5. Pass the Imaginary Object

While this activity supports all the teaching/learning concepts introduced so far, it gently challenges singers to explore yet a deeper level of imagination using mime and music. There is a direct relationship between playing games and making up music that opens the heart to improvisation in a nonthreatening way. All the groups I've worked with display remarkable enthusiasm doing this exercise regardless of their ages and musical experiences. Additionally, it introduces the idea of performing a solo for an audience and the "handoff" of the object to the next performer opens the door to the concept of motivic development. To achieve this, simply ask each new object holder to continue the previous owner's sound accompaniment, and then change it into something from their own imagination.

Participants sit or stand in a circle, and pass around an invisible object. This magical community-owned object can have whatever dimensions and weight its temporary owner desires. It can be inflated, deflated, stretchable, or malleable—whatever the owner wants it to be.

When receiving the object, each individual creates a vocal soundtrack for it. During the first few rounds, the participant should be encouraged to manipulate the object while changing the vocal accompaniment to something that best matches each motion. Later rounds might include "playing" or articulating the object as if it was a real musical instrument.

The group can assist any self-conscious performers by providing a tutti soundtrack. Give each "soloist" a time limit to "do his or her thing." Brave performers are encouraged to step into the middle of the circle or to step out and face a semicircle audience.

Activity 1.6. Human Machines

Commonly practiced in drama classes, "Human Machines" underlines the importance of listening closely to one another, and how to function as an ensemble and work together in sections of the ensemble.

I usually initiate this activity by pretending to be the face of a large clock, moving my arms and synchronizing a steady vocal "tick-tock" sound for each motion. I then call for volunteers to listen carefully for the beat source, and then slowly join in by posing as mechanical extensions of this imaginary musical device. Each individual, pair, or cluster must provide a logical, well-coordinated motion that connects to each previous mechanical installment and every gear/part must also have an accompanying vocal soundtrack that makes ensemble musical sense.

Depending on the level of musicianship and experience of the participants, these improvisations can range from simple rhythmic motifs to more complex music with reasonable rhythmic, melodic, and harmonic content.

In highly attended classes or workshops, you can divide the participants into several groups and instruct each to invent their own musical machine and ask the remaining groups to try to identify the device or at least guess its function.

In concert situations, this type of performance is perfect for audience participation. Spectators can be asked to either suggest the machine type to "stump the stars," or the performers can challenge the listeners' imagination! After twenty-five years, I have witnessed the onstage manufacture of many bionic contraptions, including some memorable washing machines, automobiles, car-wash systems, printing presses, all sorts of conveyor belted widget making devices, and even a Terminator-maker, to mention a few classic designs!

CHAPTER 2

The Groove

A "groove" in music is the rhythmic and harmonic quality of a recurring collective rhythm section pattern, over which a melody or solo is played. The groove includes drumbeats, piano or guitar comping, bass lines, and any additional accompaniment patterns played by musical instruments. It can also be achieved by a combination of instruments and vocals or simply group a cappella. A groove is the scaffold of a song upon which musical components are added, including melody and textures like background horn parts, background vocals, string "sweeteners," etc.

When I was a studio drummer, I was hired to help create rhythm track grooves along with bass, piano, and guitar players in a myriad of musical styles including pop, rock, country, gospel, Latin, jazz, R&B, funk, reggae, disco, house, and more. It was my job to know the musical components of all these styles, and very often, I had to translate what the producer or songwriter wanted into musical terms. I soon developed a much-needed vocabulary for this purpose that always began with style, feel, and tempo.

While a musical style is important to know, it is only a general description of a musical genre that, in most cases, has evolved dramatically over the years and sounds quite different from decade to decade. Therefore, to create a specific groove, the style needs to be further defined by era and artist so that the rhythm section is roughly on the same page. But the more important considerations are the time feel or "pulse" and, of course, tempo.

The word "beat" has a few meanings in the world of music. It is most often used to describe a recurring rhythmic pattern, such as a drumbeat. It also refers to the bottom note of a time signature, which indicates what kind of note value gets one beat or "count." In 4/4 time, for example, the quarter note gets one beat; a full measure is counted as "one, two, three, four." But inside each beat are smaller "pulses" that determine the time feel of a groove. These pulses are subdivisions of each beat and indicate what patterns the rhythm section will choose to play to create the feel of the groove.

There are only two beat subdivisions in contemporary popular music: duple and triple. Duple beat subdivisions basically include eighth or sixteenth notes, while triple subdivisions fall into groups of three. Both eighth-note and sixteenth-note configurations can be interpreted or "felt" as triplets (hence the label "triplet," "triplety," or "swing"). This feel is often indicated on the lead sheet. Swing feel, then, indicates that all written eighth or sixteenth notes be interpreted essentially as triplets. Swing beats in common (4/4) time are counted as "one-and-a, two-and-a, three-and-a, four-and-a."

"Straight" eighth or sixteenth feel means either rhythm should be interpreted exactly as written. In common time, straight eighth notes are counted as "one-and, two-and, three-and, four-and," while straight sixteenth rhythms would be counted as "one-e-and-a, two-e-and-a, three-e-and-a, four-e-and-a."

Duple and triple beat subdivisions are used to interpret all musical feels, so lead sheet indications might include both the style name and the time feel. Here are some examples:

- Rock straight-eighth feel
- Jazz swing eighths
- Blues 12/8 triplet feel
- Hip-hop swing-sixteenth feel
- Funk straight-sixteenth feel
- Country/pop swing-eighth feel
- Gospel "triplety" eighth feel

Activity 2.1. Alphabet Drum Set

This activity is a rhythmic interpretation of the alphabet from A to Z using eighth, triplet, and sixteenth figures. Figure 2.1 shows an example of what you can do, but you can also improvise your own version, applying different rhythms to each letter.

When improvised, this is quite an impressive way to introduce rhythms in general but also the concept of vocal percussion. Since everyone relates to the alphabet, it is the perfect introductory demonstration that segues perfectly to vocal percussion.

Suggested approaches to the "Alphabet Drum Set":

- Facilitator sings one measure at a time, participants answer (call-and-response style).
- Volunteer "soloists" sing the alphabet letters using their own rhythms while facilitator keeps a steady vocal drumbeat.
- Facilitator cues soloists to improvise on the various letters of the alphabet in sequence.

Fig. 2.1. Alphabet Drum Set

Activity 2.2. Instru-Vocal Drum Grooves

"Instru-vocal drumming" is also known as "vocal percussion." You don't necessarily need formal training to be an instru-vocal drummer, but you most definitely need to be able to keep steady time and know about the "groove." This
activity will help you develop these skills.

Figures 2.2 to 2.4 demonstrate how to instru-vocalize common drumbeats.
Note that these grooves are simplified, with only the sounds of the bass drum
(or "kick") and snare drum. Kick and snare represent the essential downbeats
of all drum grooves and are vocalized with syllables "Dn" (pronounced "doon")
and "Ka." (Hi-hat will follow.)

Track 2

Straight Eighth Feel

Fig. 2.2. Pop/Rock Straight-Eighth Feel

Track 3

Straight Sixteenth Feel

Fig. 2.3. Funk/R&B Straight-Eighth Feel

Track 4

Swing Feel

Fig. 2.4. Swing Feel

Exercise patterns in figures 2.5 to 2.7 demonstrate instru-vocal syllables that are used to imitate both ride and hi-hat cymbals used in any standard drum kit. Both cymbals are responsible for providing the steady pulse and beat subdivisions but may also be "crashed" or "splashed" to enhance accented beats. There are a variety of cymbal types that can be vocalized including ting, splash, crash, and trash cymbals to mention a few!

Track 5

Straight Eighth Feel

Fig. 2.5. Pop/Rock Straight-Eighth Feel

Track 6

Straight Sixteenth Feel

Half Open (Tss) and Closed (T) Hi-Hat

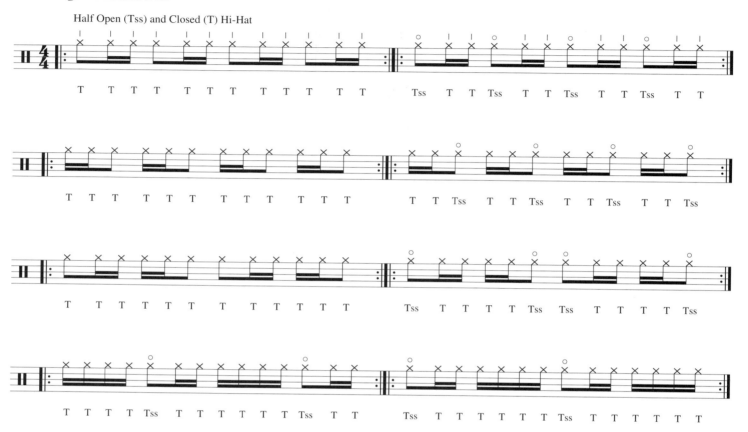

Fig. 2.6. Pop/Rock Straight-Sixteenth Feel

Track 7

Figure 2.7 demonstrates that triplets in 4/4 sound the same as eighth notes in 12/8.

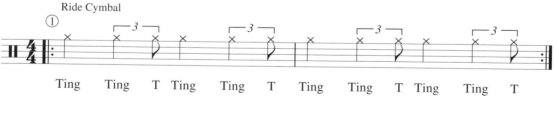

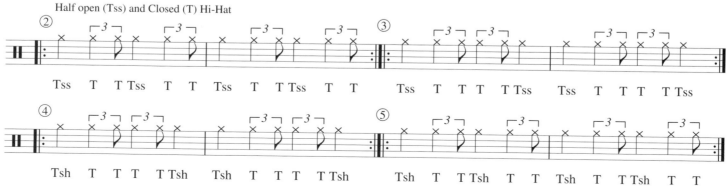

12/8 Feel

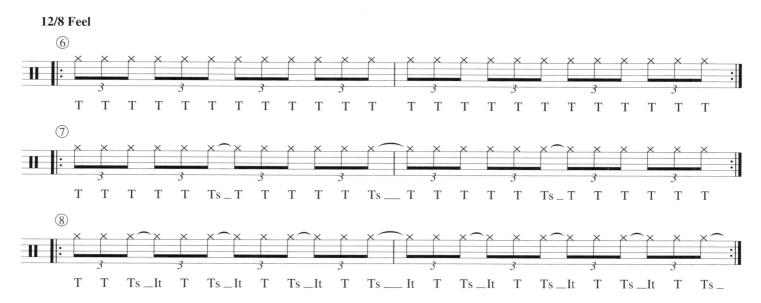

Fig. 2.7. Triplets in 4/4 vs. Eighths in 12/8

Activity 2.3. Name Game

The name game is always a crowd-pleaser, since it spotlights one of the most intimate aspects of our lives: our individual names! Our names are something we hear every day and aurally respond to our whole lives. Since names contain a variety of vowels and consonants, and sometimes multiple syllables, there are many musical ways to pronounce them. Nicknames are also good, and I recommend using your first name or nickname for starters.

I always love to start this rhythmic exercise with my own name because it has one syllable (Bob) but can be dramatically interpreted using the alphabet drum set. Figure 2.8 shows "The Name Game: Bob Song" and uses rhythms only—no pitch. The possibilities for rhythmic variation are endless, so this version is merely one of many songs I have improvised to commemorate myself!

After demonstrating your own name, request volunteers to offer their names up for rhythmic composition. Here are some suggestions for facilitators or group leaders:

- Facilitator improvises the name of the volunteer.

- Participant makes up rhythms using his/her own name.

- Several participants have a "jam session" using their names as motifs.

The Name Game
Bob Song

Track 8

Fig. 2.8. "The Name Game: Bob Song"

Activity 2.4. Multi-Name Game

Ask for a group of volunteers to stand together, side by side in a semicircle. Choose a meter, and begin conducting quarter-note beats in that meter. Then cue each participant to enter one at a time. As name motifs are introduced, draw attention to how each name "fits into" the quarter-note beat as a duple or triple rhythmic figure. Note how these motifs overlap successfully if everyone follows the conductor's beat.

Since each name has a different amount of syllables, you should wind up with some interesting polyrhythms. For those facilitators with traditional music training, think of each part as a repeating "ostinato."

A simpler version of this exercise is to have the participants rhythmically vocalize their names for a one-beat duration on cue, thus introducing the concept of improvising a solo. Then try layering the parts so that all are singing their different names simultaneously which is a perfect introduction to polyphony and counterpoint. Just make sure to hold everything together by assisting those participants who are rhythmically challenged. Even if the time feel is a bit "loose," let the singers enjoy themselves!

Activity 2.5. Melodic Multi-Name Game

This activity is the melodic/harmonic version of the previous exercise. I usually set this up by referring to how I was summoned by my family members as a child. Participants of all ages and levels have a lot of fun with this! No surprise, participants are always amazed at how many melodic variations there are for my one-syllable name, not to mention their own. Should the group want to explore this idea further, add the nicknames you were blessed (or cursed) with, as well as formal, middle, and last names.

Of course, most of our names fall into the "natural descending minor third" category. Regardless, it is a trip to listen to childhood renditions of everyone's first, middle, last, and nicknames, and realize how musical they are!

Now, of course, the name game is not limited to any particular species, so you might consider a "salute to pets" operetta, for example. Both "outer" and "inner child" have always embellished my improvisation workshops, so be open to whatever participants bring to the session. Some musical concepts to explore while engaging in this activity include tonality (major/minor), consonant and dissonant harmony, time signatures, and the groove, to mention a few.

Activity 2.6. Pitch Grooves

I got this idea from well-known vocalist Jay Clayton, a featured performer and composer in a group called Vocal Summit, which improvised most of its repertoire in live concert settings. This activity explores many aspects of a cappella group singing including harmony, tonality, blend, dynamics, articulation, attacks, cutoffs, and responding to standard (and perhaps, not so standard) conductor cues. It works best with smaller groups from four to ten singers, if you include octave and unison options.

On cue, each performer sings a pitch and continues to sustain it as the rest of the group adds their own different pitches, one by one, also on cue. Each pitch is improvised, and there are no rules to conform to regarding tonality. Once pitches are established, the participants are then asked to add a specific subdivision to a beat and tempo indicated by the leader to create a groove. For example, if the leader counts off a triplet feel in 3/4 time ("one-and-a, two-and-a, three-and-a"), each person in the group needs to create a "triplety" rhythm using their individual pitch. The combination of rhythms must groove together.

Some guidelines for this activity:

1. The first pitch can be attacked in any way, sustained with any vowel (i.e., doo, bah, zing, fleeh, soh) and articulated with any added sound effect, like vibrato, flutter-tongue, shake, etc.
2. Each succeeding singer tries to use the same attack, sustain vowel, timbre, and effect proposed by singer 1, for the purpose of establishing vocal ensemble blend.
3. In larger groups, both octaves and unisons are encouraged, but the goal is to create a chord with four to six different pitches that create consonant or dissonant harmony before rhythms are added.
4. This is a great exercise for working on intonation and rhythmic precision.
5. In order to give each member the chance to originate the chord, start with singer 1 until the chord is complete, then ask singer 2 to start, and continue until singer 1 adds the final pitch, and so on. Follow the same procedure when adding rhythms to create the final groove.
6. Mention that each initial pitch is not necessarily the root of the chord and that notes may be added above or below at random.

Variations

1. Soundtrack a suggested image or feeling as if creating a film score or background music to something.
2. Participants might try to identify the final tonality after the chord is created. Beginning-level musicians can practice just hearing consonant and dissonant chords. Intermediates might practice identifying major, minor, diminished, and augmented chord types. Advanced singers could analyze the chords in terms of sevenths and tensions.
3. The leader asks the participants to create prescribed tonalities, seventh chords, etc. If necessary, play the chord on piano first.
4. Ask the group to identify chords they have spontaneously created.
5. Play a pitch on the piano, tell the group what part of the chord it is (root, 3rd, 5th, 7th, etc.), and ask them to sing the missing pitches of the chord.

CHAPTER 3

Instru-Vocal Bass Grooves

Improvising grooves is a great way to learn a lot about the dynamics of being in a musical ensemble. One of the greatest performers of all time, Bobby McFerrin, is able to create solo grooves, and this takes enormous concentration, vocal skill, and overall musicianship. Many of his grooves include "instru-vocal" imitations of standard rhythm section instruments, including bass and drums, which support both the melody and any improvised solos. One man juggling all these musical components simultaneously with his voice is a notable accomplishment, to say the least! (I often compare Bobby to the plate spinner from the 1950's *Ed Sullivan Show* who could spin ten plates on separate poles at one time!)

But a closer examination of McFerrin's work reveals a very unique and creative approach, combining fragments of rhythm, melody (or improvisation), and harmony until the music simulates an ensemble of three or four musicians. In effect, he is able to perform as a bona fide one-man band with just his voice (and a pinch of body drumming)!

In chapter 2, we practiced some basic vocal drumbeats. Before we sing more advanced grooves, let's take a look at some basic vocal bass lines that support those drumbeats.

The fact that basses play "lines" and drums play "beats" is often misleading, as it suggests the drummer is the beat keeper of the rhythm section. The truth is that the role of bass has a bit of an edge when it comes to establishing a groove because of the instrument's rhythmic *and* melodic influence. Bass lines also define the "bottom" of the harmonic structure, so grooves will often start with a bass line, usually a one- to four-bar pattern, which keeps repeating.

For each of these bass grooves, match the style description/rhythmic feel indicated for each instrument. All are 2-measure phrases. These examples demonstrate pop/rock straight eighths, R&B straight sixteenths, and jazz swing or "triplet feel" grooves, and match the drum grooves in chapter 2. Many draw notes from the pentatonic scale (see figures 4.1 and 4.2).

Activity 3.1. Pop/Rock Instru-Vocal Bass Groove

The phrases in figure 3.1 are all pop/rock straight-eighth bass lines starting with roots and 5ths, gradually using more notes from the pentatonic scale. These bass lines will all go with the straight-eighth instru-vocal drum grooves in figure 2.2.

Track 9

Straight Eighth Feel

More Challenging

Fig. 3.1. Pop/Rock Instru-Vocal Bass Groove

Activity 3.2. Jazz/Swing Instru-Vocal Bass Groove

The swing bass lines in figure 3.2 can be performed with the swing drum grooves in figures 2.4 and 2.7.

Fig. 3.2. Jazz/Swing Instru-Vocal Bass Groove

Activity 3.3. Funk/R&B Instru-Vocal Bass Groove

The funk bass lines in figure 3.3 will work with drum grooves in figures 2.3 and 2.6.

Track 10

Fig. 3.3. Funk/R&B Instru-Vocal Bass Groove

INSTRU-VOCAL BASS AND PERCUSSION GROOVES

In the following instru-vocal bass and percussion grooves (figures 3.4, 3.5, and 3.6), note that the specific bass line rhythms do not have to coincide exactly, beat per beat, with the percussion pattern. However, the combined time feel can only be described as "in the pocket" or "grooving" when all attacks and beat subdivisions are in sync. The quality of the groove depends on how well everyone's time feel matches. The primary job of a professional rhythm section player is to be able to groove well with others in all styles or beat subdivisions.

A secondary role is to provide rhythmic and harmonic support for any additional parts, including lead and background vocals, horns, strings, etc. These parts are "layered" to create a musical arrangement and are visually presented as a full written score or as a "lead sheet." But before adding any parts to the groove, let's first "tighten up" our time feels by practicing these grooves.

Activity 3.4. Pop/Rock Bass and Percussion Groove

Fig. 3.4. Pop/Rock Bass and Percussion Groove

Activity 3.5. Jazz Swing Bass and Percussion Groove

Fig. 3.5. Jazz Swing Bass and Percussion Groove

Activity 3.6. Funk/R&B Bass and Percussion Groove

Fig. 3.6. Funk/R&B Bass and Percussion Groove

Adding Motifs to the Groove

Once the groove is established, either the leader may assign additional motifs or singers can spontaneously improvise parts to create what is sometimes called a "circle song," because everyone stands in a circle. Participants should be encouraged to make musical decisions and take risks at all times!

LAYERING PARTS OVER THE GROOVE

Perhaps the best user-friendly scale for improvisation is the pentatonic scale, because all notes of this 5-note scale can be improvised or layered without fear of dissonance. All you need are rhythmic variations and assorted compositional techniques of choice, exemplified in "Groove in G." Layering spontaneous parts that work well together is what group improvisation is all about!

Activity 3.7. "Groove in G"

"Groove in G" is also the intro to a piece I wrote called "Ooh-Yah" (see the appendix) that was recorded by the European a cappella group, Vocal Summit, and later by a Boston-based band called "The Ritz." This groove uses a pentatonic ostinato bass line with layered parts that also use notes from the pentatonic scale (see figure 4.1). "Groove in G" can be played with piano accompaniment or sung a cappella. The following is an analytical breakdown of each section:

Sections A and B introduce a G pentatonic bass line supported by a GMaj6 chord played on piano and/or vocal layers. The background vocal might be introduced one part at a time until all three parts are sung simultaneously. Practice using intervals, scale-step numbers, or solfege syllables. Learning background vocal parts requires at least two out of these three pitch-learning approaches.

Section C uses the same pentatonic voicings but with "concerted" rhythms, which are rhythmically articulated simultaneously.

Section D spells the notes of the pentatonic chord by articulating them as "bell-tones." Staggered entrances will help improvisers hear the chord tones they will be using to improvise solos. This section uses the "oo" vowel for sustained pitches but can be varied. Students will learn how to count and subdivide by practicing this section.

Section E uses some different counterpoint pentatonic figures before the open solo section (section F). Note that even more parts may be added or existing layers doubled, depending on the size of the group. We shall explore how to improvise a solo using the pentatonic scales (and others) in the next chapter.

Section F is the solo section, "open" to any of the designated singers to improvise. Simply use the notes of the pentatonic scale with various rhythms. In chapter 4, we will examine some specific melodic patterns for the pentatonic scale (and other scales) that can be used to practice soloing.

Track 11

Groove in G

Fig. 3.7. Groove in G

Basic Scales for Improvisation

Melodic improvisation requires familiarity with a variety of both traditional and contemporary scales and how to use them to navigate through a sequence of chords, called a "progression." After learning the correct pitches of a scale, the second step is to practice articulating different melodic note sequences. The additional application of beat subdivisions or "time feels" allows musicians to practice these sequences using a straight or triplet interpretation.

Let's examine some basic patterns using the pentatonic scales, Dorian mode, and blues scale.

PENTATONIC SCALES

Track 12

The *major pentatonic scale* is a 5-note scale (introduced in activity 3.7, "Groove in G") that uses major scale degrees 1, 2, 3, 5, and 6 (Do, Re, Mi, Sol, and La).

Fig. 4.1. C Major Pentatonic Scale: Do to La

Track 13

Note that the relative-minor pentatonic has the same notes but starts on 6 (La). Minor pentatonic is a choice scale to use on minor or minor 7 chords. Degrees 4 and 7 (Fa and Ti) are both absent from the pentatonic scale, which makes it a perfect starting place for beginning improvisers.

Fig. 4.2. A Minor Pentatonic Scale: La to Sol

Activity 4.1. Pentatonic Patterns

Track 14

These phrases are built from pentatonic patterns. They will work harmonically with both the C major and A minor chords. In the eighth-note patterns, each phrase may be interpreted with a swing or straight feel.

Fig. 4.3. Scalar Patterns

Activity 4.2. Pentatonic Patterns against Chords

Track 15

Figure 4.4 is an example using C major, while figure 4.5 exemplifies A minor. Either chord will work to accompany each exercise, but the patterns in 4.4 center more on the note C as the tonal center, while 4.5 revolves more around the note A. Note the addition of scat syllables and articulation markings for short (^) or accent (>). If you prefer, feel free to invent your own scat syllables!

Fig. 4.4. Straight Eighth Feel

Track 16

Straight Sixteenth Feel

Fig. 4.5. Straight Sixteenth Feel

Activity 4.3. Pentatonic Bass Lines

Track 17

Minor pentatonic bass lines need to start on and return to scale degree 1 or 6 often enough to suggest the relative major or minor tonality, since the scale notes of A minor pentatonic and C major pentatonic are the same.

Straight or Swing Sixteenth Feel

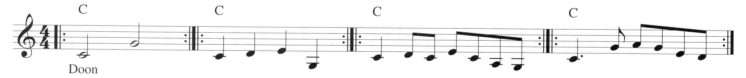

Straight Sixteenth Feel

Fig. 4.6. Minor-Pentatonic Bass Lines

Now, let's take a listen to a few other choice scales when improvising over a minor chord.

DORIAN MODE

Track 18

The Dorian mode is like a major scale with lowered scale steps 3 and 7. We can also think of Dorian as the notes of a major scale moving diatonically from degree 2, or from "Re" to "Re," up the octave.

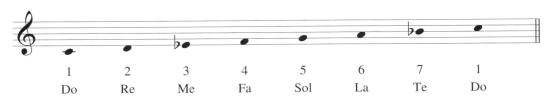

Fig. 4.7. C Dorian as Related to Major

Track 19

Figure 4.8 illustrates C Dorian as a separate modal scale, starting and ending on step 2 (Re to Re) of B♭ major. Either way you analyze it, you have a Dorian tonality that is often used to improvise solos over minor chords. While the harmonic, melodic, and natural-minor scales are similar, the Dorian mode has its own special flavor because of the natural 6th scale step (La).

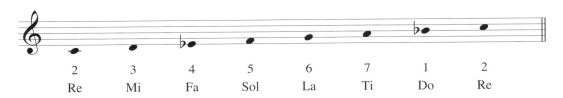

Fig. 4.8. C Dorian as a Modal Scale

Activity 4.4. C Dorian Patterns

Track 20

Figure 4.9 is a scalar pattern exercise in C Dorian.

Fig. 4.9. Dorian Practice Patterns

Activity 4.5. Three Dorian Solos

Track 21

Figure 4.10 includes 8-bar Dorian solos over C–7 with different time feels. (The sixteenth-feel solo is only four bars in length.) Invent your own syllables for examples 2 and 3!

Straight Eighth Feel Solo

Swing Eighth Feel Solo

Straight Sixteenth Feel Solo

Fig. 4.10. Three Dorian Solos

Activity 4.6. Dorian Patterns

Track 22

Figure 4.11 includes some instru-vocal bass lines in C Dorian. While these lines are written in treble clef, you should sing them in any octave or key of your choice.

Straight or Swing Eighth Feel

Doon

Straight Sixteenth Feel

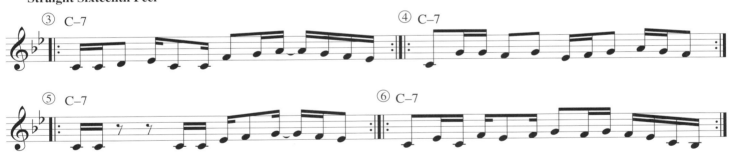

Fig. 4.11. Dorian Bass Lines

THE BLUES SCALE

The blues scale (figure 4.12) can be used to improvise over many progressions that include both major and minor chords. It can be thought of as a minor pentatonic scale with a flat 5th degree.

| 1 | ♭3 | 4 | ♭5 | 5 | ♭7 | 1 |

Fig. 4.12. C Blues Scale

Activity 4.7. Blues-Scale Patterns

Track 23

Practice these patterns derived from the blues scale. Use your own syllables.

C Blues-Scale Half Notes

Fig. 4.13. C Blues-Scale Patterns, Half Notes

Track 24

C Blues-Scale Quarter Notes

(Use C7 or C–7)

Fig. 4.14. C Blues-Scale Patterns, Quarter Notes

Track 25

Straight Eighth Patterns

(Use C7 or C–7)

Fig. 4.15. C Blues-Scale Patterns, Eighth Notes

Track 26

Triplet Patterns

(Use C7 or C–7)

Fig. 4.16. C Blues-Scale Patterns, Triplets

Track 27

Straight Sixteenth Patterns

(Use C7 or C–7)

Fig. 4.17. C Blues-Scale Patterns, Sixteenth Notes

Activity 4.8. Blues-Scale Solos

Sing the 12-bar blues solos with different grooves in figure 4.18. Note key changes and some of the jazz articulations used in these examples.

Track 28

Fig. 4.18. C Major Blues Practice

Track 29

② **D Blues Scale**

Swing Eighth Feel

Fig. 4.19. D Minor Blues Practice

Track 30

③ **A Blues Scale**

Straight Sixteenth Feel

Fig. 4.20. A Major Blues Practice

INTEGRATING MINOR PENTATONIC, DORIAN, AND BLUES SCALES

So far, we have explored each of these scales as separate tonal centers and interpreted patterns using them with duple or triple subdivisions (aka "feels"). Parts of these scales can also be combined, as long as they relate harmonically to the chord.

Fig. 4.21. D Minor Pentatonic, Dorian, and Blues

Activity 4.9. Integrated Scale Patterns

Track 31

Figure 4.16 demonstrates the integration of minor pentatonic, Dorian, and blues scale patterns. All of these patterns function over minor chords.

Fig. 4.22. Scale Practice, Straight Eighth Feel

Track 32

8-Bar Solo with Swing Eighth Feel

Fig. 4.23. Scale Practice, Swing Eighth Feel

Track 33

4-Bar Solo with Straight Sixteenth Feel

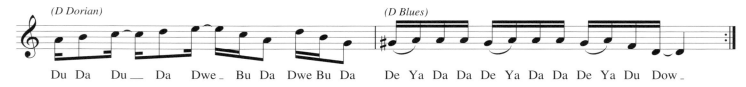

Fig. 4.24. Scale Practice, Straight Sixteenth Feel

Activity 4.10. Integrated Scale Solos

The blues scale will also work over the dominant 7 chords used in major blues progressions, as exemplified in figure 4.17, even with the natural 3rd in the tonal center's dominant 7 chord (D7).

Track 34

12-Bar Blues in D

Fig. 4.25. Blues in D

Activity 4.11. Integrated Dorian and Minor Pentatonic

Dorian mode and minor pentatonic are best reserved for minor chords, as exemplified in figures 4.26 and 4.27. Figure 4.26 also uses natural minor (or Aeolian mode) in measures 4 and 5, which uses flat 3, flat 6, and flat 7. The indicated scat syllables allow for smooth melodic articulation (as in previous solo examples), but feel free to use your own syllables if you already have a "knack" for scat!

12-Bar Blues in C Minor

Track 35

Fig. 4.26. Blues in C Minor

Activity 4.12. Harmonic Minor Solo

Note the use of the harmonic minor scale in figure 4.27 on the E dominant 7 in measure 9. We will take a closer listen to dominant 7th chords shortly. Try to invent your own scat syllables!

Track 36

Blues in A Minor

Fig. 4.27. Blues in A Minor

Activity 4.13. "Blue Yah"

Now back to group improvisation for a minute, this time using a minor version of the song "Ooh Yah" called "Blue Yah." Note the bass line now includes a flat 7 but no third. This allows us to use the minor pentatonic, Dorian, and blues scales, which all have a flat 3.

This arrangement is a perfect example for practicing solo development using pentatonic, blues, Dorian, natural minor, and harmonic minor scales over a minor chord vamp. My scale of choice for minor 7 chords happens to be Dorian mode, because I like the natural 7th degree of the scale. The piano part is for additional harmonic reference as needed. The piece was originally intended to be performed a cappella. You could also perform it with piano, bass, and drums. Solo sections over G–7 may be added anywhere in the arrangement.

The word "vamp" indicates that the section may be repeated indefinitely.

Two people may perform the vocal percussion parts (VP 1 and VP 2) or just one person can sing (VP 3).

Blue Yah

To Coda ⊕

Repeat and Fade

2nd time D.S. al Coda

Fig. 4.28. "Blue-Yah"

Scat: The Voice as a Musical Instrument

RHYTHMIC PHRASING

One of the most important considerations in vocal improvisation is how to articulate notes. The voice is a musical instrument (hence the term "instru-vocal"), but unlike others, it must produce notes and resonate without the help of sticks, bows, reeds, or mouthpieces. The solution is to use instru-vocal text, commonly known as "scat" syllables that simulate the articulations of more customary musical instruments, especially horns.

Activity 5.1. Scat Phrases

The rhythmic exercises in figures 5.1 to 5.3 exemplify common scat syllable combinations with different time feels in 1-bar, 2-bar, and 4-bar phrases. Note the different articulation indications (markings) on some specific note values. For example, the quarter note is sometimes articulated with just an accent (>) and other times shortened (^) to sound just a bit "fatter" than a staccato interpretation.

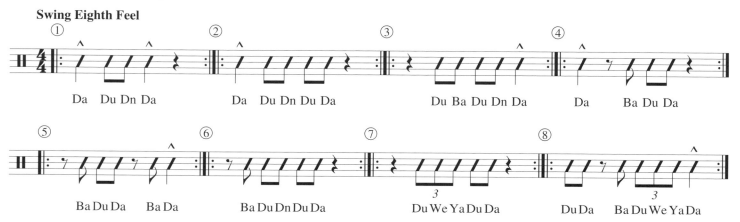

Fig. 5.1. 1-Bar Phrases

Swing Eighth Feel

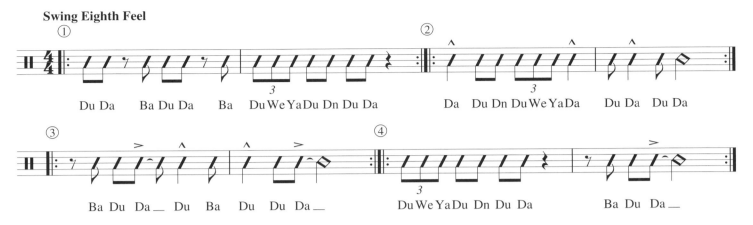

Fig. 5.2. 2-Bar Phrases

Straight or Swing Sixteenth Feel

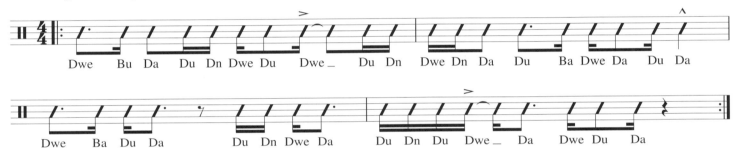

Fig. 5.3. 4-Bar Phrase

Activity 5.2. Scat Solos

Figures 5.4 and 5.5 are 8-bar solos punctuated with four separate phrases.

Straight or Swing Eighth Feel

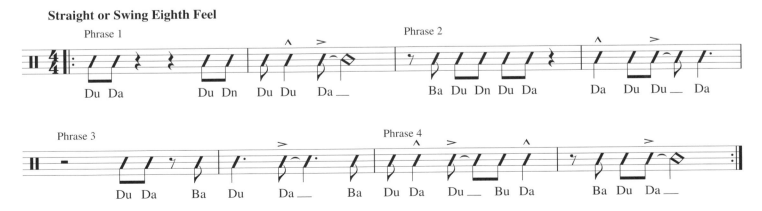

Fig. 5.4. Scat Practice Solo 1

Straight or Swing Sixteenth Feel

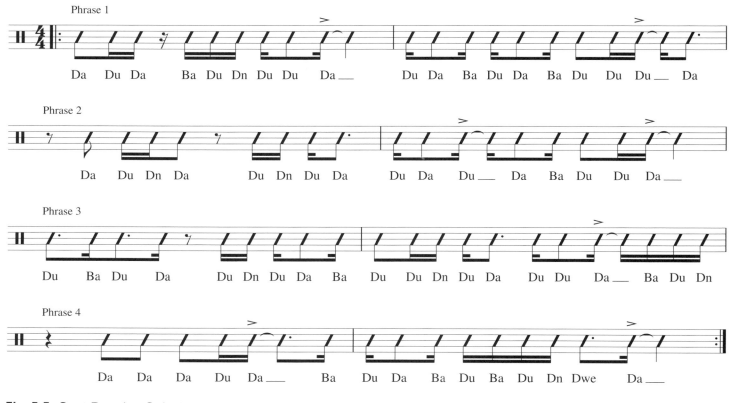

Fig. 5.5. Scat Practice Solo 2

Figure 5.6 is a 16-bar solo divided into four phrases.

Straight or Swing Eighth Feel

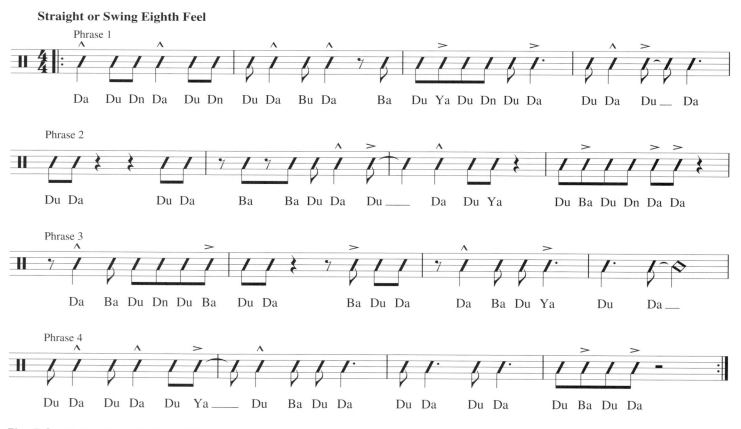

Fig. 5.6. 16-Bar Solo in Four Phrases

Figure 5.7 is a 12-bar solo divided into three phrases.

Straight or Swing Eighth Feel

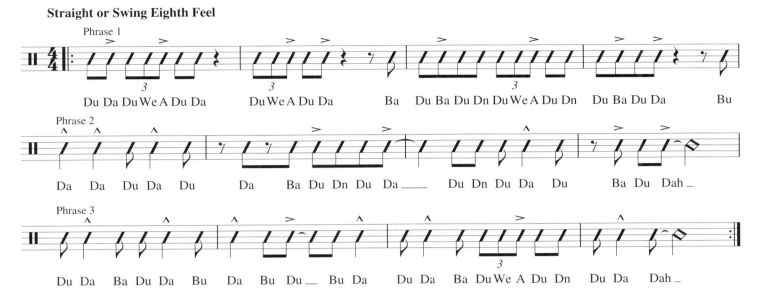

Fig. 5.7. Scat Practice Solo 3

Activity 5.3. Scat with Pitch

By adding pitch, the art of scat singing presents another level of challenge for the improviser. Since we've been exploring minor tonality, figures 5.8 to 5.10 contain 1-measure and 2-measure phrases in different time feels over D minor. Some notes in these scat phrases have articulation markings that indicate accent (>) or short (^), as in previous examples.

Practice each example in call-response style by first "saying" the syllables in rhythm, without pitch, and then singing them with designated pitches. I sometimes refer to this rhythm-only technique as "spoken scat," since it involves nonpitched vocal articulation of rhythmic figures.

Track 38

Straight or Swing Feel

Fig. 5.8. 1-Bar Pentatonic Phrases

Track 39

Straight or Swing Sixteenths

Fig. 5.9. 1-Bar Dorian Phrases

Track 40

Fig. 5.10. 2-Bar Blues Phrases

Activity 5.4. Stories

Since musical phrases are like sentences in a narrative, think of groups of phrases as paragraphs representing a sequence of cohesive ideas that tell a story. Scat singing is just another form of musical commentary that uses rhythm, melody, and pitch—much the same as any musical instrument does. For me, scatting is a bit "closer to home," because it utilizes spoken language and is articulated by the human voice. I think of a scat solo as a musical narrative with vocal inflection, punctuation, poignant pauses, and the development of cohesive ideas.

With that in mind, let's take a look and listen to the scat solo in figure 5.11, which is a 12-bar blues form divided into three 4-bar phrases, punctuated by occasional pauses. Note that phrases don't necessarily end when there is a pause or even a chord change. Divvy up the phrases as you prefer; 2-bar, 4-bar, or longer; it doesn't really matter. I find it practical to think of making three statements of four bars each, but only after having practiced and examined the song's theoretical elements, like identifying and hearing roots, guide tones, chord scales, articulations, etc. This way, a solo becomes much more than just an application of these musical elements.

I have discovered that most people are able to do this with very little training in music theory. Space is just as important as notes, so let's look at the next example that exemplifies less symmetric phrasing with longer pauses in between them.

Track 41

Fig. 5.11. 12-Bar Minor Blues Solo

Activity 5.5. Tortoise Shell Samba

"Tortoise Shell Samba" includes a solo section over a single dominant 7th chord. Originally a solo bass line created by bassist Wayne Pedzwater (Buddy Rich, Paul Simon), "Tortoise Shell Samba" was the first composition I recorded featuring my particular style of scat singing known as "multi-instru-vocal." The solo section was cast over a dominant 7 chord, and we decided to keep all six vocal solo tracks because each stood alone but also worked perfectly when played simultaneously with the other solo takes. The solo section in the final mix sounded like a Swingle Singers jam session!

Here's a breakdown of its sections.

INTRO: Originally an improvised electric bass line, the introduction can be sung or played on piano or both. The piano part in the score was added just for cues but could enhance the performance, depending on the harmonic support needs of the ensemble.

A Tenors 1 and 2 state the melody first time; altos 1 and 2 add a nice harmony on the repeat.

B The GMaj6 tonality is set up for letter C, which is a "bell-tone" background. The B section may be performed as is or behind scat solos. (Use the pentatonic scale for any solos.)

C A brief interlude or optional solo section, again using the G pentatonic scale.

D This is the officially designated solo section with a tonality of G dominant 7, as indicated by the piano cues. We're going to explore some options for improvising over a dominant 7 chord in the next section.

E This interlude briefly departs from the key of G using horn-like vocal bell tones to outline the chord changes. This could also be used as a solo section for more advanced groups.

Track 42

Tortoise Shell Samba

Fig. 5.12. Tortoise Shell Samba

DOMINANT 7 CHORDS

To improvise over the D section of "Tortoise Shell Samba" (figure 5.12), we need to take a look at some scale options for dominant 7 chords. Like the Ionian (major scale) and Dorian modes, Mixolydian is also a diatonic scale, but beginning on step 5 (Sol). Or, we can alter any major scale with a flat 7th degree to make it Mixolydian mode.

Figures 5.13 to 5.15 illustrate the construction of the Mixolydian mode in the keys of G and C. Note that some of these examples are sung an octave lower on the recording. Sing them in your most comfortable range.

Track 43

Sol   La   Ti   Do   Re   Mi   Fa   Sol   Fa   Mi   Re   Do   Ti   La   Sol

Fig. 5.13. G Mixolydian Mode in Key of C

Track 44

Do   Re   Mi   Fa   Sol   La   Te   Do   Te   La   Sol   Fa   Mi   Re   Do

Fig. 5.14. G Major Scale with Flat 7

Alternatively, the C Mixolydian scale in figure 5.15 can be thought of as being in the key of F (which has one flat) but starting on the 5th degree.

Track 45

1   2   3   4   5   6   7   1   7   6   5   4   3   2   1

Fig. 5.15. C Mixolydian

Activity 5.6. Mixolydian Patterns

Figures 5.16 to 5.18 demonstrate quarter note, triplet, and straight-eighth patterns, with "slur" articulations using letters "w" and "y." Note the placement of vowel sounds "ah," "eeh," and "ooh" in each exercise. As a general rule, I prefer "ah" and "ooh" for lower notes and "eeh" for higher notes, when articulating melodic patterns.

Fig. 5.16. Quarter-Note Slurs

Track 46

Fig. 5.17. Triplet Slurs

Track 47

Fig. 5.18. Eighth-Note Slurs

Activity 5.7. Mixolydian Solo Ideas

Figure 5.19 offers twelve 2-bar phrases using the Mixolydian mode over G dominant 7. Feel free to use these ideas in the 1-chord solo vamp section of "Tortoise Shell Samba."

Track 48

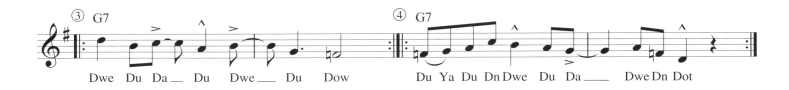

Fig. 5.19. Solo Ideas

CHAPTER 6

Team Improvisation

A choir is like any other community that works together to reach a common goal. In the case of vocal improvisation, the objective is to create spontaneous ideas that are cohesive, aesthetic, and make musical sense. So far, we have explored both intuitive and theoretical components of improvisation using mostly a group format, but with additional rhythmic, melodic, and harmonic considerations for soloing. Many of the group exercises discussed in the previous chapters are designed to instill self-confidence, encourage a willingness to take risks, and raise the level of nonjudgmental trust in one's own creative ability. Once these comfort zones have been reached, it is time for the group members to consider more intimate interaction to reach a higher level of artistic expression. This may sound simple, but in my experience as a teacher, eye contact alone is a formidable prospect to most novice and even intermediate-level improvisers. So, here's an "eye-opener" that will definitely encourage team spirit, cooperation, and creativity!

Activity 6.1. Mirror Image

This exercise is commonly used in drama classes and may be applied appropriately to group vocal improvisation. It can be performed with any reasonably sized group. I've facilitated groups ranging from six to forty students!

1. Form two lines so that all participants are standing face-to-face, one-on-one. Designate line 1 as the "leaders," and ask them to move very slowly using mostly their arms and hands, but to remain relatively sedentary. Any motions may be paused or continuous but should be performed at a slow pace so they are easy to follow. Designate line 2 as the "followers" this round, and have them mimic their partners' movements to create a "mirror image." Note that mirroring can be in parallel or contrary motion (same or opposite direction). The important lesson here is cooperation. This first exercise is performed in silence in order to focus on and strengthen visual communication skills.

2. Now exchange the roles of leader and follower between the two lines, with line 2 leading.

3. Begin the exercise again, but first announce that during this round there are no designated leaders or followers—rather, a continuum of motion where both partners share the control equally. This takes a lot of cooperation to be successful! In addition, facilitators can get a bird's-eye view of the personalities in the group, as some folks will tend

to dominate while others remain passive. This game is a terrific process for each personality type to learn to temper their natural inclinations. Remember to maintain a slow momentum at all times, especially during this round.

Repeat the exercises with alternate partners so that everyone gets a chance to interact with all other members of the group. To achieve this, I will often command the group to "freeze," "remix" (find new partners), and "continue on cue." If the lines are long, make sure to meander and visit each team to check on their progress. If there are chaotic moments, let the participants have some fun, particularly if they've never done this kind of thing before. Later, you can always discuss what worked or didn't and why.

Activity 6.2. Musical Mirrors

Adding a musical component to mirror imaging makes sense when you consider the importance of musicians bonding in any group format, from piano trios to a 16-piece jazz big band to a 70-piece concert orchestra! Collective improvisation demands a high level of cooperation in order to be successful, especially in larger groups. It requires that the performers be willing to share control of all musical creations by exchanging the roles of leader and follower. It is also an effective way to temper any egocentrism that inevitably emerges within musical co-ops. Remember that each face-to-face pair is a team and is expected to work together.

Begin rhythmic and/or melodic ideas with team 1 and continue sequentially through the two parallel lines, one pair at a time. Each team contributes a rhythmic and/or melodic pattern that also works harmonically with all patterns previously initiated. Additionally, the music may be derived from the body movement or vice versa.

Here's how to initiate musical mirrors:

Step 1.   Team 1 coordinates a movement and eventually adds a vocal musical pattern that matches their physical motions (or vice versa, starting with a musical motif instead). One or both of these ideas can be spontaneously improvised by the participants or offered by the facilitator, should there be an attack of shyness or hesitation. The duration of each motif should be one to two measures and adhere to the initial groove.

Step 2.   The primary groove (initiated by team 1) should continue for a while before the additional teams add their own motifs, adding layer upon layer to the groove. I suggest doing this slowly, adding one team at a time sequentially. While this is taking place, the facilitator should visit each team and draw attention to the tonality, time signature, and beat subdivision as necessary to make the combined effort as musical as possible. Once team 1 is singing and moving, invite team 2 to layer a different musical motif and also link their musical pattern with a corresponding body movement.

Keep moving down the line always making sure that all parts make musical sense. If there is a discrepancy with the rhythm, meter, beat subdivision, or tonality, the facilitator should use the "erase" signal (see chapter 7, "Hand Signals"), and then ask the particular team to re-invent something more musically congruous. Explain why the part was incompatible, either at the time or afterward. Remember that in this exercise, body movement is of secondary importance, so there is no need to qualify, synchronize, or "correct" any motions in any way.

Activity 6.3. Ice Sculptures

This is a very creative and artistic exercise for all levels, but make sure your group is comfortable with physical contact. Several teams of four or more create a group image or design but remain motionless, as if posing for a photo shoot. The music may be created before or after the pose, but the image and music should match.

With still life imagery, the music is very often slow and sometimes angelic, but not necessarily. Remember that the goals of this exercise include bonding, cooperation, and building community through music.

Variations:

1. One group creates musical accompaniment to a different group's pose ("picture"). I call this "Freeze-Frame Film Composing."

2. The entire group or several groups create musical accompaniment to pictographic images. (An excellent source is commercial posters.)

3. The group improvises musical accompaniment to a select video in the same way that a composer creates a film score.

Several years ago, I had the opportunity to work with a fantastic group of mostly Italian singers during a vocal improvisation workshop in Bologna, Italy. The event took place at Club Bentivoglio, a grotto restaurant offering great food, wine, and entertainment. At first, I thought this was an odd place to hold a workshop, but soon discovered it was a haven for musical creativity. Part of our final public performance included most of the musical activities described in this book. The entire concert was an exceptional demonstration of spontaneous vocal improvisation, in particular, the musical accompaniment we created to the photos, paintings, and frescos that decorated the cavernous walls of this improvisation wonderland.

Activity 6.4. The Singing Wheel

Here's a good one if you're rehearsing on a carpeted floor or a nice quiet lawn space outdoors. Participants lie on their backs forming a wheel with all heads in the center, face up. In this position, everyone can hear each other quite well but unable to make any eye contact. Motifs are open to the first vocal bidder, and additional parts are layered ad hoc as the music evolves.

Outdoor improvisations can be special events if you luck out with some interesting cloud configurations, street noises (e.g. car horns), and things with wings.

CHAPTER 7

Advanced Group Improvisation

In order for group improvisation to succeed, it is important that all participants feel comfortable initiating, changing, and embellishing musical motifs. These skills are also essential for the facilitator in order to demonstrate communication techniques that will enable the ensemble to function autonomously. Advanced groups will be able to perform without a conductor, as all participants are trained to "lead" and "follow" each other spontaneously.

Without music or conductor cues, autonomous group improvisation requires specific gestures so that teams are able to communicate their intention to change the music. This is easier than it sounds, although I recommend training for high-level groups with previous ensemble experience since they are familiar with some standard cues. The following exercises work well in a circular or semicircular format:

Activity 7.1. Hand Signals

First, establish a three-team groove with two to four singers on each team. Assign a different melodic pattern to each team (advanced participants can make up their own motifs), but hold off on adding harmony within the team so that each team is singing a different unison line (octaves are okay).

Step 1. Demonstrating Hand Signals

Demonstrate some standard cues for controlling dynamics and tempo. To cue legato, I often make fluid motions simulating the bowing of a violin. For staccato, I like to use shorter, abrupt motions like tweezing your fingertips rhythmically. Finally, use the cut-off cue (right hand counterclockwise circle, finger close at end of circle) for "erasing" or removing a part. All participants should learn these three simple articulation cues, which will be used to alter the music during actual performances.

Step 2. Organize Teams

Take a group with a similar configuration of three to four teams, and assign a number to each singer. For example, in a group of nine, three teams of three singers should be sequenced in threes—for example, 1-2-3, 1-2-3, 1-2-3. Teams of four would be sequenced 1-2-3-4, 1-2-3-4, 1-2-3-4, and so on.

Have the group form a semicircle or full circle. Ask all the 1's from each team to come to the center and stand back-to-back, facing their teammates (say, singers 2, 3, 4 of each 4-person team). Announce that all number 1s are the captains of their teams and that they will be responsible for initiating all prime motifs.

Step 3. Start the Groove

The 3- to 4-part improvisation begins in the center of the circle starting with the captains. As soon as the first motif begins, ask the other captains to listen and wait, while you draw attention to the groove.

Prime motifs set up the tempo, beat subdivision, and sometimes harmony for the groove—particularly if there are thirds and sevenths in the line; these harmonic considerations should be emphasized to make sure everyone is on the same page. Traditionally trained musicians will undoubtedly react differently than contemporary jazz and popular musicians, but the bottom line is to create mindful music.

Once the captains establish a 1- or 2-measure ostinato groove approved by the facilitator, they physically return to their teams, and each team continues to sing their part in unison.

Step 4. Changing Dynamics and Articulation

Ask the captains to cue their teammates to sing loud, soft, staccato, and legato. Encourage other musical cues of choice.

Step 5. Diminution and Augmentation

Ask the captains to shorten their team's ostinato using the hand signal for "erase." This can apply to the first, middle, or last part of a motif. Once the erase gesture is made, the captain maintains the quarter-note beat but with a closed fist, which means, "count but don't sing during these beats." This takes some practice but will come naturally to those who compose music because it is much the same as writing and editing a composition, but live and direct.

In addition, the captains have to be mindful (or "earful") at all times by listening closely to all the other teams who are also changing their motifs, eventually doing this concurrently.

After all teams have entered their motif, go very slowly, one team at a time, and ask each team to shorten their motif, using the gesture for "erase." Team 1 shortens their part, while the remaining teams keep singing their original motif until cued by the facilitator to change. Make sure to draw the attention of the team captains to the specific change, pointing out the rhythmic and/or melodic (later on harmonic) space that has been created. Team 2 then shortens their part while everyone continues. Team 3 repeats this procedure, and so on through the last team.

Repeat this process until the captains eventually reduce their individual team part to one beat of pitch and/or rhythm. The facilitator makes sure the group maintains a steady beat at all times. Counting rests is a great way to practice different meters and improve both individual and cooperative time-keeping.

Continue this procedure with the number 2s as team captains, then all the number 3s as captains, etc., until everyone has had a chance to lead their group. Then try the same exercise using augmentation or extending the motif. Start with a few notes and give each captain a turn at slowly adding notes to their motif.

SPECIFIC HAND SIGNALS

Dynamics: palm(s) up for loud, reverse for soft. Use mirrored hands open and closed for sforzando, crescendo, and decrescendo.

Articulation: close fingers for staccato, arco motion (bowing) for legato.

Pitch Bending: (includes glissando, slide, spill, doyt, falloff, trill, and shake) use the snake motion, arm and hand for slow (e.g., gliss), and flap hand for faster articulations (e.g., the shake or trill).

Rhythmic Variation

Sometimes, a motif will spontaneously include a salient rhythmic pattern of interest. For example, in common time, a measure consisting of two eighth notes on beat 1 followed by three beats' rest can be varied by using numeric representations, in this case by cueing repetitions with fingers. The new rhythms will replace the former rests. Showing one finger could mean one quarter- or eighth-note duration, while two to five or more fingers (using two hands) indicate those repetitions. Specific rhythms (any combination of eighths, triplets, and sixteenths) are simply demonstrated by physical conductor-type cues. Three fingers, for example, could mean three eighth notes, a triplet, or two sixteenths with an eighth.

Each captain needs to indicate how the rhythm is to be interpreted by tapping each finger in the desired rhythm or any other way that is obvious to their teammates.

Activity 7.2. The Improv Ferris Wheel

This is one of the pinnacles of group improvisation for more advanced musicians or seasoned group improvisers. This format requires constant singing, physical motion, and motif variation. The role of captain keeps rotating so that all have the opportunity to be in charge. Teams keep changing their configurations throughout the exercise so that every participant gets to interact with all of the other group members. This works best with nine, twelve, fifteen, or sixteen singers (teams of three or four). For the sake of this discussion, I will be using a 12-member group.

Divide the group into four teams of three members. Assign numbers to each team in sequence (1-2-3, 1-2-3, 1-2-3). Ask the 1s to enter the center of the circle, stand back-to-back, and face their teammates (the 2s and 3s).

Captains then create compatible, facilitator-approved motifs, which they pass on to their teammates using hand signals. After the groove settles, captains (1s) shift their positions one or two steps to the left so that they are now facing a neighboring team of 2s and 3s. Captains stop singing at this point while the 2s and 3s continue the motif invented by their previous captains.

The 2s and 3s teach their new 1 captain the team motif. The new captain abandons his/her former motif and learns the new one by following cues, motions, and hand signals indicated by the new team.

Once the captains learn the new motif, they begin initiating changes using techniques described above including erasure, diminution, augmentation, etc.

Remember that this is all taking place simultaneously among the four teams, so the captains are responsible for listening like hawks to the music going on around them at all times.

All changes to the various parts should be monitored and approved by the facilitator to insure the integrity of the groove. If the groove becomes too cluttered or "busy," by all means, use staccato or erasure to shorten or even remove a part completely. Space (rest) is very often a good thing, as it can clear any clutter and create room for new musical ideas.

Keep rotating captains until a full circle has been made and the captains are once again facing their original teammates. At this point, all 2s replace 1s and begin their service as captains.

Continue until all participants have led all teams. Remember that in this exercise only captains can initiate musical changes. The facilitator calls out when to switch captains.

Activity 7.3. Adding Choreography

Choreography is another dimension of creativity that complements vocal improvisation utilizing skills learned in the previous mirror-image exercises. If you are fortunate to have any dancers in your group, make sure to induct them into the role of team captain!

In circle or semicircle format, create teams without choosing leaders. Natural leaders always emerge by virtue of personality, experience, and comfort zone—in this case, those who are dancers, or at least comfortable with body movement.

Once the groove is set, ask each team to add a motion to their motif. The natural movers will usually jump right in with a motion that complements their team's particular motif and the music as a whole. These motions should be monitored and edited by the facilitator, as needed. In terms of specific movements, footsteps are often represented by rhythmic ideas while arms and hands frequently signify melodic contour, articulation, and musical expression. Facilitators may have to help out on this one, but more often than not, kids—especially high-school level—will jump right in with confidence and glee!

Sometimes, two singers on the same team will initiate a movement simultaneously. In this case, I help out by choosing the better of the two motions or call for the initiators to quickly reach agreement, especially if neither gives in to the other. But this is all part of learning how to work together as a team, so I usually let the architects work it out, and they do.

Remember that the learning process is just as important as the final performance, if not more so. Improvisation is not premeditated or prescribed, but it can be practiced, and the process of creating spontaneous music is something to behold! Many group performances under my direction are intentionally presented as snapshot works in progress (or improvisation in real time). Audiences always appreciate the process as much as the final product.

Activity 7.4. "Bait and Switch" Improvisation

In this circle-format game, there are no specific teams or captains but rather temporary leaders of constantly changing teams. This exercise may be practiced sitting down or standing. It's a terrific exercise in musicianship but also transcending the ego. If there are any hidden personal disparities within the group, this exercise will exorcise them rather quickly! For groups that will be together for a while, this is especially highly recommended. All groups should avoid drawing attention to the psychodramas that may unfold.

Begin with a call for a motif, open to the first volunteer motivator. No problem if two motifs are initiated simultaneously, but more than three or four motifs, and the music will sound cluttered. The first time you do this, start with one rhythmic or melodic motif. Once this has been established and facilitator approved, welcome anyone in the group who likes this motif to sit (or stand) next to that person and join in by singing in unison or adding harmony.

Next, call for a second motif, to be initiated by any member of the group who hasn't joined the first motif. Interested singers should join this second team as desired. Eventually, all participants will be part of three or four teams, each committed to a specific musical motif.

Now the fun begins! All participants keep an "open ear" to the music being created around them, and the rule is not to stay with any team/motif for too long. So, while a participant is singing unison or harmony with one team, he or she is simultaneously scanning for another motif of interest being offered by another team in the circle. Once a selection has been made, the participant migrates to the team of interest, which must make room for the new teammate. The mover has the option of "bumping" someone out of a team by tapping their knee or shoulder, and the "bumpee" must comply and quickly find another team to join.

A rule to follow: if anyone tries to initiate a new motif and no one joins in, that person must either coerce someone to join them or abandon the motif and join another team. This is where egocentrism sometimes emerges, but who ever said cooperation and building community was easy?

Once the participants are familiar with the process, reasonably secure with their own musical abilities, comfortable with each other socially, and promise not to take their expressive whims too seriously, this exercise can be a unique journey into uncharted musical realms! But if noncompliance is taken personally, you may have to console a wounded ego or two. One remedy for this situation is to apply rule 2: Anyone who finds himself or herself singing alone must immediately assume the role of soloist, move to the center of the circle, and improvise over the groove!

Soloists are always welcome and encouraged to "take center circle." Confident soloists are also entitled to initiate cues to the others in order to regulate tempo, dynamics, and articulations. One way to encourage soloists is by tapping them on the shoulder and leading the person to the center of the circle. Each soloist follows suit by tapping someone else when they are done. Shy solos will most likely be short, while confident solos may go on too long. Facilitators should use cues for "keep going, you're doing great!" or "great job, but time for someone else's turn."

WORD GAMES

This unique approach takes group improvisation up yet another notch! It utilizes the combination of music and text—a technique in jazz known as "vocalese." Vocalese is attaching words to every note of a solo line, as Annie Ross did in her version of "Twisted," which was originally a saxophone solo played by Wardell Gray. With group word games, however, both text and music are improvised simultaneously to create a groove. So a bass line, vocal percussion, horn articulation—pretty much anything—can have text added.

There are two ways to initiate musical word games:

1. Let words evolve naturally from scat syllables, or

2. Improvise music to text.

Deriving words from scat lines is pretty easy to do, considering the linguistic nature of scat singing. Sing a syllabic phrase over and over, and after a while, it starts to sound like comprehensible text. This applies to all languages, of course. In fact, when working with singers from different countries, I liven up this game by suggesting participants use their own native language. Sometimes I don't even know what the participants are singing about, but they always seem to be having a good time!

Activity 7.5. Text Improvisation: 1-Part Inventions

The concept of text improvisation began years ago with a T-shirt one of my group participants was innocently wearing during a rehearsal. Although I don't remember what was written, you can easily imagine the abundance of labels, quotes, and logos displayed on T-shirts and sweatshirts that people wear these days.

With that in mind, let's begin with a simple example using local colleges in the Boston area of Massachusetts:

Berklee College of Music (my alma mater and my former employer) comes to mind first, of course! But let's examine the intrinsic rhythmic possibilities hidden in this very famous 4-word multisyllable logo. Figures 7.1 to 7.7 demonstrate different rhythmic interpretations of the Berklee College text.

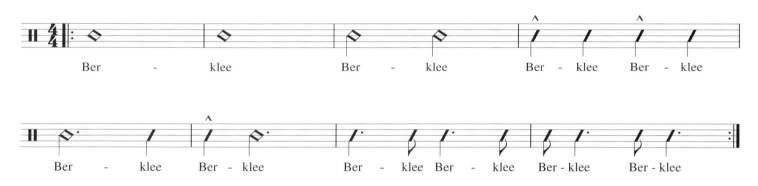

Fig. 7.1. Berklee

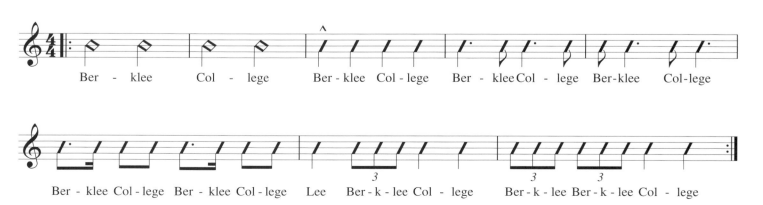

Fig. 7.2. Berklee College

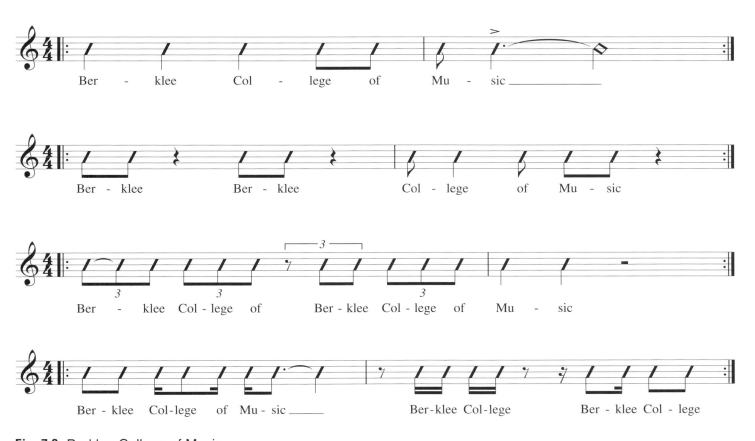

Fig. 7.3. Berklee College of Music

Figure 7.4 applies the major pentatonic scale.

Track 49

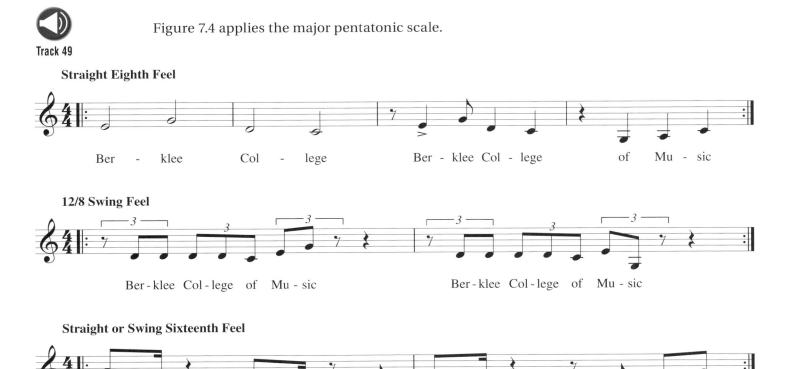

Fig. 7.4. Pentatonic

Track 50

Figure 7.5 exemplifies both rhythms and pitches from the Dorian mode.

Straight Eighth Feel

12/8 Swing Feel

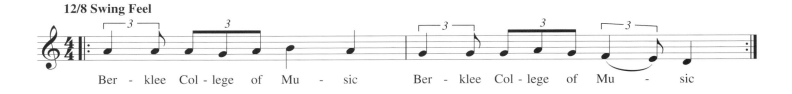

Straight or Swing Sixteenth Feel

Fig. 7.5. Dorian

Track 51

Figure 7.6 uses notes from the blues scale.

Straight Eighth Feel

12/8 Swing Feel

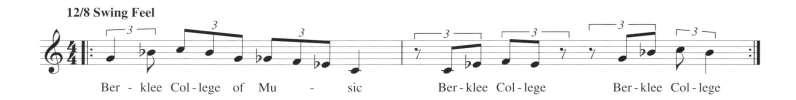

Straight or Swing Sixteenth Feel

Fig. 7.6. Blues

Track 52

Figure 7.7 utilizes the Mixolydian mode.

Straight Eighth Feel

Ber - klee   Col - lege   Col - lege   of   Mu - sic

12/8 Swing Feel

Ber - klee   Col - lege   of   Mu - sic   Ber - klee   Col - lege   of   Mu - sic

Straight or Swing Sixteenth Feel

B - B - B   Ber - klee   Col - lege   Col - lege   of   Mu - sic

Fig. 7.7. Mixolydian

Track 53

Figure 7.8 demonstrates other names of colleges in the Boston area set to different grooves and tonalities.

Straight or Swing Sixteenth Feel (D Dorian)

Mid - dle - sex Com-mun - it - y   Mid - dle - sex Com - mu - nit - y Col - lege

Swing Feel (F Pentatonic)

Fram - ing - ham   I   go   to   Fram - ing - ham   State

Straight Eighth Feel (D Mixolydian)

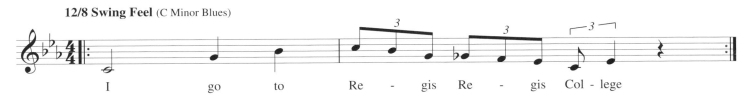

Bent - ley   Bent - ley   Bent - ley   Col - lege

12/8 Swing Feel (C Minor Blues)

I   go   to   Re - gis   Re - gis   Col - lege

Fig. 7.8. Other Colleges

Rhythmic and melodic variations depend on stylistic interpretation and the groove. But any text will fit into a continuum of quarter, eighth, triplet, and sixteenth rhythms, especially when punctuated by rests.

Activity 7.6. 2-Part Inventions

Let's examine some 2-part inventions for voices in treble clef using different states located in the United States. These are 2-measure grooves built on major and minor blues, major and minor pentatonic, and Dorian and Mixolydian tonalities. My daughter came up with the alto motif in figure 7.9 when she was eleven years old. I took this theme with me to the Idaho Jazz Festival when I taught improvisation workshops there in 2009. Kids have a natural knack for this kind of thing when they're not feeling self-conscious or pressured.

Track 54

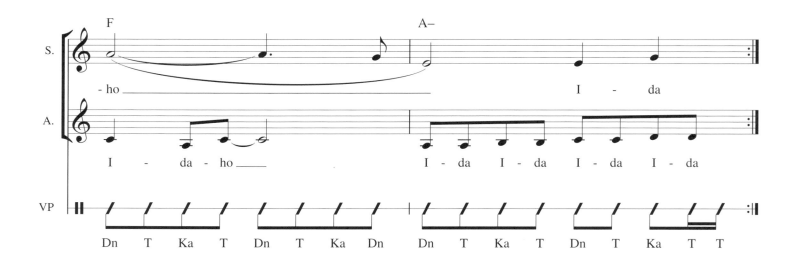

Straight Eighth Half-Time Feel

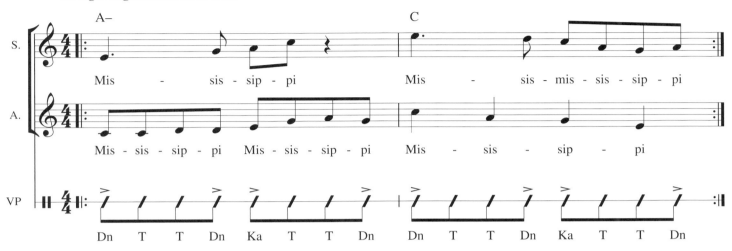

Swing

Straight or Swing Sixteenth Feel

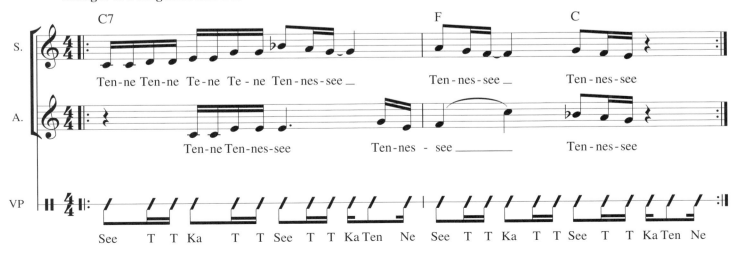

Straight Eighth Feel

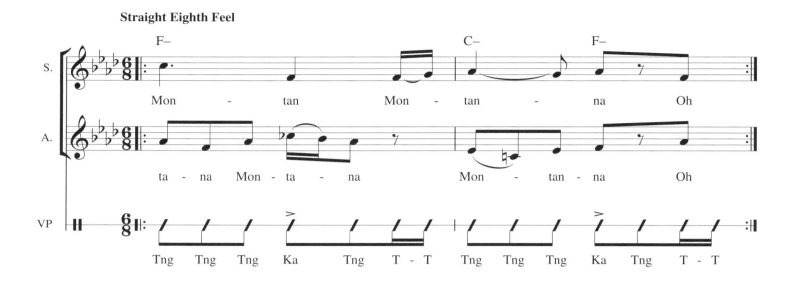

Waltz Feel in 6/8

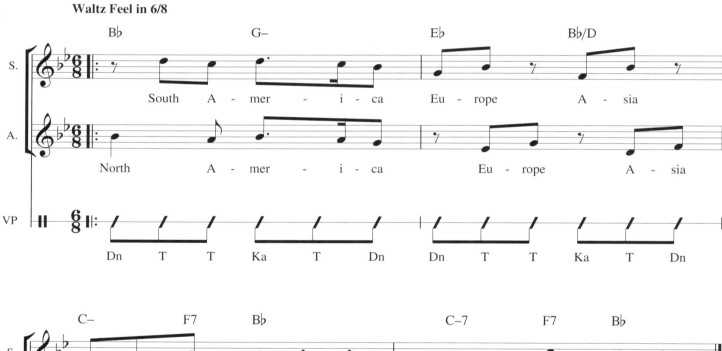

Fig. 7.9. 2-Part Inventions [3 pages]

Activity 7.7. Multipart Inventions

Now let's take a look at some multipart inventions using a variety of food and drink options. Menus are a perfect source for improvisation. Often, I will pass one (or several) around, and let each team choose the entrée, beverage, or dessert they prefer—even during live concert performances. Once choices are made, each team goes into a "huddle," and the first to emerge with a motif establishes the groove of the improvisation.

Note that grooves don't have to start with a bass line. They can be initiated from any ensemble perspective.

Make sure to draw attention to the starting team so that all ears are focused on the rhythm and tonality of the opening motif. If two teams initiate motifs simultaneously, the facilitator chooses the team with the strongest groove, and the "bumped" team must respond with a supportive theme as quickly as possible. At any time, if a team adds a motif that doesn't work musically with all the other parts, give them the "erase" cue and reveal the cause of the musical incongruity, especially during rehearsals or workshops. In concert situations, this is a great process for the audience to observe, so often I will explain how initial motifs are improvised and why final parts are subject to approval.

In figure 7.10, different texts have been layered instead of using the same text for all three motifs. The VP beat is more of an accompaniment part and not necessary if you want all your participants to sing melodic motifs.

Pizza Toppings

Track 55

Coffee Drinks

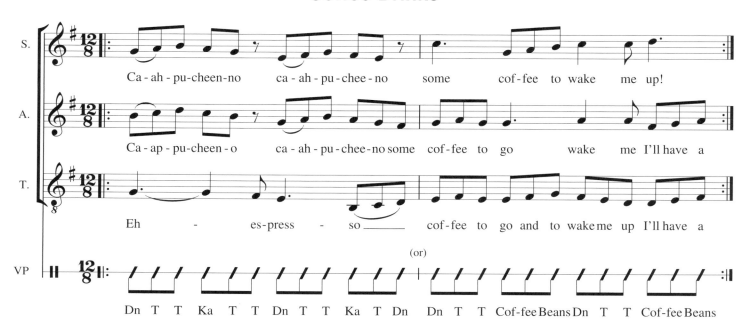

Traffic Signs

Chinese Food

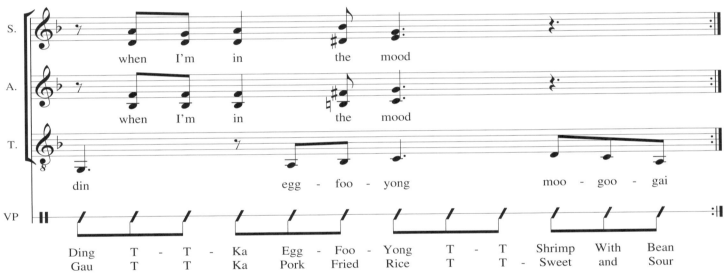

Sports Samba

Fig. 7.10. Multipart Inventions

CONCLUSION

After perusing *Vocal Improvisation*, it should be evident to readers that vocal improvisation has evolved significantly since Louis Armstrong began to scat sing during his recording of "Heebie Jeebies," back in 1921. The story—perhaps a fable—was Louis either dropped the music or forgot the lyrics. Whether serendipitous or intentional, Louis Armstrong deserves credit for being one of the first jazz musicians to articulate the voice like a musical instrument. Louis played what he sang and sang what he played on the horn. And if he were alive today, I'm sure Louis would be impressed with the remarkable progress and achievements made by his successors who have brought vocal improvisation to its current summit.

The impetus for writing this book stemmed from the group improvisation activities I have been using at workshops and seminars. My experience has revealed that an instru-vocal approach, especially for group improvisation, applies to all ages and levels of musical proficiency when carefully facilitated. Since many of the exercises may seem a bit vague when reading the verbal descriptions above, I would like to encourage readers interested in group improvisation to visit my website to view actual recorded workshop footage of the games and exercises described in the beginning and latter portions of this book.

Students, teachers, and professional singers who want to improve their solo improvisation competencies will find this book extremely helpful by regularly practicing the rhythmic and melodic patterns, exercises, and phrases. I also want to encourage vocalists to listen to instrumentalists improvise and try to emulate the various ways players articulate their solos. Remember to listen and practice, and most of all, experience the joy of vocal improvisation!

APPENDIX

Ooh Yah

Track 56

Fig. A.1. Ooh Yah (Advanced)

ABOUT THE AUTHOR

Photo by Martin Weiskoff

Bob Stoloff is a distinguished educator, conductor, clinician, and choir/big band/combo adjudicator of jazz festivals throughout the United States, Canada, South America, and Europe. For many years, he was a professor and administrator at Berklee College of Music. His unique and comprehensive workshops include traditional scat singing, spontaneous group improvisation, and vocal/body percussion. Bob has three other publications available entitled *Scat! Vocal Improvisation Techniques*, *Blues Scatitudes* (Gerard/Sarzin), and *Body Beats* (Advance Music). He teaches online courses in vocal improvisation and vocal percussion at www.studyjazzonline.com, where videos are available of improvisation games such as those discussed in this book. He is currently chair of the voice department at Instituto de Musica Contemporanea, Universidad San Francisco de Quito, Ecuador.

More Fine Publications from Berklee Press

WOODWINDS

SAXOPHONE SOUND EFFECTS
by Ueli Dörig
50449628 Book/CD $14.99

FAMOUS SAXOPHONE SOLOS
arr. Jeff Harrington
50449605 Book $14.99

IMPROVISATION FOR FLUTE
by Andy McGhee
50449810 Book $14.99

IMPROVISATION FOR SAXOPHONE
by Andy McGhee
50449860 Book $14.99

FOLK INSTRUMENTS

BEYOND BLUEGRASS
Bluegrass Fiddle and Beyond
by Matt Glaser
50449602 Book/CD $19.99
Beyond Bluegrass Banjo
by Dave Hollander and Matt Glaser
50449610 Book/CD $19.99
Beyond Bluegrass Mandolin
by John McGann and Matt Glaser
50449609 Book/CD $19.99

IMPROVISATION SERIES

BLUES IMPROVISATION COMPLETE
by Jeff Harrington
Book/CD Packs
50449486 B♭ Instruments $19.95
50449488 C Bass Instruments $19.95
50449425 C Treble Instruments..........$22.99
50449487 E♭ Instruments..................$19.95

A GUIDE TO JAZZ IMPROVISATION
by John LaPorta
Book/CD Packs
50449439 C Instruments $19.95
50449441 B♭ Instruments $19.99
50449442 E♭ Instruments $19.99
50449443 B♭: Instruments $19.99

BERKLEE PRACTICE METHOD

BERKLEE PRACTICE METHOD
With additional volumes for other instruments, plus a teacher's guide.
Bass
by Rich Appleman, John Repucci and the Berklee Faculty
50449427 Book/CD $14.95
Guitar
by Larry Baione and the Berklee Faculty
50449426 Book/CD $14.95
Keyboard
by Russell Hoffmann, Paul Schmeling and the Berklee Faculty
50449428 Book/CD $14.95
Drum Set
by Ron Savage, Casey Scheuerell and the Berklee Faculty
50449429 Book/CD $14.95

WELLNESS

MUSIC SMARTS
by Mr. Bonzai; edited by David Schwartz
50449591 Book $14.99

MANAGE YOUR STRESS AND PAIN THROUGH MUSIC
by Dr. Suzanne B. Hanser and Dr. Susan E. Mandel
50449592 Book/CD $29.99

THE NEW MUSIC THERAPIST'S HANDBOOK – SECOND EDITION
by Dr. Suzanne B. Hanser
50449424 Book $29.95

MUSICIAN'S YOGA
by Mia Olson
50449587 Book $14.99

MUSIC THEORY/EAR TRAINING

REHARMONIZATION TECHNIQUES
by Randy Felts
50449496 Book $29.95

ESSENTIAL EAR TRAINING FOR THE CONTEMPORARY MUSICIAN
by Steve Prosser
50449421 Book $16.95

BEGINNING EAR TRAINING
by Gilson Schachnik
50449548 Book/CD $14.99

BERKLEE MUSIC THEORY – 2ND EDITION
by Paul Schmeling
50449615 Book 1: Book/CD $24.99
50449616 Book 2: Book/CD $22.99

MUSIC BUSINESS

MAKING MUSIC MAKE MONEY
by Eric Beall
50448009 Book $26.95

MUSIC LAW IN THE DIGITAL AGE
by Allen Bargfrede and Cecily Mak
50449586 Book $19.99

HOW TO GET A JOB IN THE MUSIC INDUSTRY – 2ND EDITION
by Keith Hatschek
50449551 Book $27.95

MUSIC MARKETING
by Mike King
50449588 Book $24.99

THE FUTURE OF MUSIC
by Dave Kusek & Gerd Leonhard
50448055 Book $16.95

THE SELF-PROMOTING MUSICIAN – 2ND EDITION
by Peter Spellman
50449589 Book $24.95

MUSIC PRODUCTION & ENGINEERING

MIX MASTERS
by Maureen Droney
50448023 Book $24.95

PRODUCING IN THE HOME STUDIO WITH PRO TOOLS – THIRD EDITION
by David Franz
50449544 Book/DVD-ROM $39.95

RECORDING AND PRODUCING IN THE HOME STUDIO
by David Franz
50448045 Book $24.95

PRODUCING AND MIXING HIP-HOP/R&B
by Mike Hamilton
50449555 Book/DVD-ROM $19.99

PRODUCING DRUM BEATS
by Eric Hawkins
50449598 Book/CD-ROM Pack $22.99

PRODUCING & MIXING CONTEMPORARY JAZZ
by Dan Moretti
50449554 Book/DVD-ROM $24.95

FINALE: AN EASY GUIDE TO MUSIC NOTATION – 3RD EDITION
by Thomas E. Rudolph and Vincent A. Leonard, Jr.
50449638 Book $34.99

UNDERSTANDING AUDIO
by Daniel M. Thompson
50449456 Book $24.99

SONGWRITING, COMPOSING, ARRANGING

COMPLETE GUIDE TO FILM SCORING – 2ND EDITION
by Richard Davis
50449607 ....$27.99

THE SONGWRITER'S WORKSHOP
by Jimmy Kachulis
50449519 Harmony: Book/CD $29.95
50449518 Melody: Book/CD $24.95

ARRANGING FOR LARGE JAZZ ENSEMBLE
by Dick Lowell and Ken Pullig
50449528 Book/CD $39.95

MUSIC NOTATION
THEORY AND TECHNIQUE FOR MUSIC NOTATION
by Mark McGrain
50449399 Book $24.95

MUSIC NOTATION
PREPARING SCORES AND PARTS
by Matthew Nicholl and Richard Grudzinski
50449540 Book $16.95

SONGWRITING: ESSENTIAL GUIDE
by Pat Pattison
50481582 Lyric and Form Structure: Book ...$16.95
50481583 Rhyming: Book..................$14.95

JAZZ COMPOSITION
by Ted Pease
50448000 Book/CD $39.99

MODERN JAZZ VOICINGS
by Ted Pease and Ken Pullig
50449485 Book/CD..................$24.95

MELODY IN SONGWRITING
by Jack Perricone
50449419 Book/CD..................$24.95

MUSIC COMPOSITION FOR FILM AND TELEVISION
by Lalo Schifrin
50449604 Book $34.99

POPULAR LYRIC WRITING
by Andrea Stolpe
50449553 Book $14.95

HAL•LEONARD® CORPORATION
7777 W. BLUEMOUND RD. P.O. BOX 13819 MILWAUKEE, WI 53213

Prices subject to change without notice. Visit your local music dealer or bookstore, or go to **www.berkleepress.com**

1111

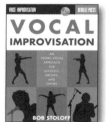
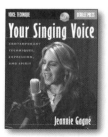

U.C.B.